FOR YOUR HOME

FIREPLACES & HEARTHS

FOR YOUR HOME

FIREPLACES & HEARTHS

CANDACE ORD MANROE

Little, Brown and Company
Boston   New York   Toronto   London

Dedication

For Meagan and Drew

First Edition

ISBN 0-316-54756-5

Library of Congress Catalog Card Number 94-75951

A FRIEDMAN GROUP BOOK

10 9 8 7 6 5 4 3 2 1

Published simultaneously in Canada by Little, Brown & Company (Canada) Limited

FOR YOUR HOME: FIREPLACES & HEARTHS
was prepared and produced by
Michael Friedman Publishing Group, Inc.
15 West 26th Street
New York, New York 10010

Editor: Sharyn Rosart
Art Director: Jeff Batzli
Designers: Patrick McCarthy and Lynne Yeamans
Photography Editor: Jennifer Crowe McMichael
Production Associate: Camille Lee

Color separations by Fine Arts Repro House Co. Ltd.
Printed and bound in China by Leefung-Asco Printers Ltd.

Table of Contents

INTRODUCTION

A quick scan of the real estate ads in any newspaper's classified section is revealing: After the number of bedrooms and baths included in a home's vital statistics intended to induce a prospective buyer's interest often appears this denotation: WBFP (wood-burning fireplace). The message couldn't be clearer: The fireplace is a beloved, much sought-after feature—so important, in fact, that it is one of the key influences in the winnowing process of selecting a home. For many homeseekers, if a fireplace is not part of the package, an otherwise ideal location and floor plan become meaningless.

Perhaps the visceral appeal of the fireplace is atavistic, a carryover from the days of early humans, who learned to use fire for warming, cooking, and clearing out land. Even though a fireplace today is rarely a prerequisite for survival, the flames it represents may still have the effect of fostering a sense of safety, security, and general well-being.

It may be that the fireplace touches an even deeper, more mysterious taproot. Perhaps the mesmerizing crackle and sizzle, sweet-smelling woodsmoke, and enchanting fluidity of the ever-changing spectrum of the fire represent the unknown, the inexplicable magic of nature in its most elemental form, igniting a state of primal wonder in the beholder.

One fact, at least, is beyond dispute: It's easy to get lost in fire. And it's not surprising that so many of us desire to do just that, insisting that our homes come equipped with the opportunity.

Hearth and home have been linked throughout history for more than alliterative reasons. The hearth—the floor of the fireplace that juts out into a room—has become synonymous with the heart of the home, the nucleus of warmth and nurturing that makes the home a safe haven.

In the first permanent homes built in England and Europe, the fireplace was located in the kitchen, a multifunctional space also known as the "hall" or "keeping room." These fireplaces were originally referred to as chimneys, which explains the references found in literature of that time to the

Left: THE WEATHERED PATINA AND PAINT OF THIS FIREPLACE'S CARVED WOODEN MANTEL LEND A SENSE OF WARMTH AND AN OLD-WORLD AMBIANCE TO THIS DINING ROOM.

"chimney corner" as the place where the family gathered. These early fireplaces were immense structures spanning eight to ten feet in width and extending six feet in both height and depth. At first, ovens weren't built into the fireplace, so all cooking was done directly over the fire. A heavy wooden lug pole rested high up within the fireplace, supporting the pothooks from which the kettles were hung. Later, bake ovens (known as beehive ovens because of their shape) were built into the fireplace structure, in a separate bricked-in space that jutted out just to the upper left of the main fireplace opening and shared a side wall with the main fireplace. Below the bake oven, in the same brick extension, was the ash oven, where ashes were stored. Because the fireplace was a source of heating as well as cooking, the room around it was cozily arranged with high-back settles—early sofa-like benches—drawn close to the hearth to capture the heat and block out drafts.

By the seventeenth century, the fireplace and its hearth remained the safest, warmest, and most sociable place in the home—the center for the preparation of meals, the source of heat, and the gathering place for the family. This was true of simple, everyday houses and folk-style peasant dwellings in Scandinavia and much of Europe, England, and even colonial America. To best fulfill its function, the fire-

place was prominently situated in the center of the home. Today, when journeying through old New England towns and villages, one can't help but notice the central chimneys, square and ruggedly sturdy, bisecting the rooflines of historic homes in the same fashion as those of the English cottages that were their precursors.

As home life became increasingly sophisticated, so did the fireplace. As one of the major architectural features of the home, the fireplace reflected the popular architectural style of its time, changing in appearance according to the prevailing design preference. For example, in America, after the War of Independence, the neoclassical style known as Federal design dominated, and the large, rustic fireplace of the colonial era was replaced with a smaller, more refined structure. The Federal fireplace alluded to Britain's neoclassical Georgian architecture with a mantelpiece of flanking wooden pilasters topped with an entablature that was delicately carved then painted. Other period architectural styles and design movements brought their own brand of style to the fireplace, from the French Rococo, English and American Victorian, Arts and Crafts (a movement started in the late nineteenth century by William Morris in England), to Bauhaus, which originated in Germany in 1919 and spread throughout Europe and America.

Above: ALTHOUGH TRADITIONAL IN APPEARANCE THANKS TO THE WOOD CONSTRUCTION OF THE MANTEL AND ITS WHITE PAINT, THIS FIREPLACE DEVIATES FROM HISTORICAL PRECEDENCE WITH ITS CANTILEVERED PYRAMIDS SUPPORTING THE MANTELSHELF AND WITH THE FLARED EDGES OF THE FIREBOX.

Today, the fireplace can take virtually any form, depending on the design preference of the homeowner. It can reflect the owners' proclivity for period design: In new country homes, for instance, it's not unusual for the fire-

place to take the capacious, primitive style of the colonial epoch. The mantelpiece can range from ornate and curvaceous, reflecting a fondness for the French rococo style, to a sleek, white concrete or marble plane with a small rectangular opening that serves as a pronouncement of minimalist contemporary design.

In addition to identifying a historic period or design style, the fireplace can be an indicator of regional style, from Southwestern adobe to Adirondacks fieldstone. With today's freedom of expression in interior design and its resulting one-of-a-kind artistry in all facets of decor from furnishings to floor coverings, the fireplace is also becoming, in many homes, a whimsical expression of singular creativity. Such a fireplace pays homage to no design school, period, or region, but honors only the vision of the creator, taking flights of fantasy, just for fun.

In all of its variations, the fireplace is an integral part of the home. Not only is it an important architectural element that undergirds the interior's design, but it also is a forum for expressing the personalities of the homeowners. Symbolizing warmth, security, contentment, mystery, fellowship, and even romance, the fireplace, to be fully understood, must be seen as a fixture of the heart as well as of the home.

The Fireplace: Yesterday and Today

Besides being a cozy addition to any home, the fireplace is a clue to the home's place in history. In dating a home, architectural historians rely on the fireplace as a key piece of evidence. Its architectural and construction styles, as well as its building materials, enable dating the fireplace to a period, if not a precise year.

In many primitive European homes and in the early New World homes of the colonial era, fireplaces were large brick or stone structures not uncommonly spanning the entire room in width. More functional than decorative, these primitive fireplaces were adorned only with a simple wood mantelshelf—or, perhaps, a raw timber—used to display the family's pewter or china. The fireplace's large size, though important in providing a bountiful heat source, existed primarily for cooking purposes: Large slabs of meat could be roasted, whole, in the capacious space directly over the coals.

Fireplaces changed according to the increasing sophistication of the society. Their appearance varied from country to country, depending on the available building materials and the specialized skills of the artisans. In the Ukraine, for example, where hand-glazed tiles were an indigenous craft, fireplaces were ornamented with distinctive blue and white tiles, similar to those of the Netherlands. As the colonists adapted to life in the New World, building more sophisticated dwellings, their fireplaces also became more refined. Simple wooden mantelpieces, usually painted some variation of blue, green, or gray with natural-pigment buttermilk paints, graced the more stately homes.

In the eighteenth century, England's Georgian style, with its roots in classical Rome, permeated home architecture and design throughout the British empire. Fireplaces reflected this neoclassicism with elaborate carving. A Queen Anne interior from around the 1730s might have featured a fireplace conceived as a piece of Roman architecture, with columns, reinterpreted as pilasters, supporting an architrave, frieze, and molded cornice. Instead of a mantelshelf, the Queen Anne fireplace might have had a pan-

Left: Baking ovens cut into one side of the front of the fireplace quickly became a standard feature of the colonial fireplace. Prior to this development, all cooking was done directly over the flame. A bit more elegant than some of the very early fireplaces, this one features a plain paneled mantel, rather than a primitive hewn beam.

eled chimney breast and fireplace surround, with flanking cockleshell cupboards (Baroque devices).

In America, the Federal period of the late eighteenth century introduced more of a national character to Georgian architecture and a somewhat lighter touch to the fireplace style—notably, white woodwork carved in linear, neoclassical motifs. At this time, the heavy carving of the Georgian period's fireplace gave way to a delicate bas-relief decoration, which was often appliquéd using French putty.

By 1830, the Roman influence in neoclassical architecture had been preempted by that of ancient Greece. For the fireplace, the Greek Revival style meant a decorative wooden structure that was both practical and ornamental—and painted exclusively in white. The nineteenth century's Industrial Revolution, with the increased manufacturing and availability of building materials that accompanied it, resulted in a rash of eclecticism in architecture. Homes took any number of historical antecedents as their design style, from Gothic (Gothic Revival thrived for several decades around the middle of the century) to Georgian and even Egyptian style. This architectural diversity meant that fireplaces varied significantly from one home to the next, despite the age of the home. While Victorian homes from the mid-1800s were a celebration of eclecticism, with many fine examples con-

structed in styles such as Italianate and French Empire, the prevailing image that sticks in memory from these homes is one of opulence; for the fireplace, that translates as opulently carved mantelpieces, usually in stained, not painted, wood. As a reaction to the fussiness of Victorian design and the Industrial Revolution, the Arts and Crafts Movement at around the turn of the century rebelled against too much decoration, relying on quality materials and fine but understated handcraftsmanship to achieve its unique style. Arts and Crafts fireplaces were often made of stone, some with etched inscriptions of ideals, others featuring hand-glazed tiles, hammered copper accents, or the Mission style's famous golden oak, simply carved and hand-assembled.

In the twentieth century, the most notable architectural style to leave an indelible influence on the fireplace is Bauhaus, or the International, style. Sleek and modern, fireplaces conceived in this school of design are stripped of ornamentation, presented as flat plaster, marble, or concrete, with the fireplace opening itself appearing as only a small rectangle, perhaps irregularly positioned in an asymmetrical design.

In new homes today, fireplaces can draw from a wealth of historic styles to communicate mood or to re-create a sense of the past.

Above: In colonial America's early permanent homes, fireplaces were utilitarian architectural features essential for a family's survival, providing both heat and an area for preparing food. These primitive fireplaces were wide and deep enough to accommodate the hearth cooking of large game, and they were constructed of indigenous building materials, often fieldstone.

Right: THIS EARLY FIREPLACE SUGGESTS EUROPEAN ORIGINS, CUT INTO A SIMPLE WHITEWASHED WALL AND CAPPED WITH A HAND-HEWN BEAM AS A MANTEL-PIECE AND ITS ONLY ORNAMENTATION. THE STARK SIMPLICITY AND PERFECT SYMMETRY OF THE FIREPLACE DESIGN ARE ENDURING QUALITIES THAT MAKE IT A SOURCE OF BEAUTY AND EMULATION TODAY.

Right: THE COLONIAL-STYLE FIREPLACE IS NOT LIMITED TO HISTORIC ARCHITECTURE. WITH THE ESCALATING POPULARITY OF COUNTRY DESIGN, PRIMITIVE STYLE FIREPLACES ARE REAPPEARING IN NEW HOMES MODELED AFTER THE COLONIAL ERA. THE DISTINCTIVE PERIOD FEATURE OF THIS FIREPLACE IS ITS BAKE OVEN NICHE ON THE LEFT SIDE.

Left: THIS CONTEMPORARY INTERPRETATION OF A COLONIAL FIREPLACE IS SMALL ENOUGH TO FIT COMFORTABLY INTO A MODERN KITCHEN-DINING AREA, WHERE IT BRINGS AN OLD-FASHIONED WARMTH TO COMPLEMENT THE COUNTRY-STYLE DECOR AND FOLK-ART ACCESSORIES.

Above: As the function of the fireplace changed, and it became exclusively a purveyor of heat instead of also acting as a cooking source, the fireplace's form changed correspondingly: It became smaller and more ornamental. **Right:** With its roots in classical architectural principles, the eighteenth century's prevailing aesthetic resulted in fireplace designs that were heavily carved. Their mantelpieces often included ornate pediments that rose above the fireplace mantel, blending into an entire room design that was conceived as a celebration of ancient architecture.

Right: AS A TESTAMENT TO ONE OF THE MOST PRODUCTIVE DESIGN PERIODS OF ALL TIME, THE EIGHTEENTH-CENTURY FIREPLACE BRINGS CLASSIC STYLING TO ANY ROOM, ESTABLISHING A REFINED, TRADITIONAL CHARACTER THAT CAN EASILY BE CARRIED FORTH IN COMPLEMENTARY FURNISHINGS.

Above: THE EIGHTEENTH CENTURY'S REVIVAL OF CLASSICAL ARCHITECTURAL FEATURES IS EVIDENCED BY THIS FIREPLACE'S DENTIL MOLDING SET BENEATH AN ENTABLATURE, AND ITS FLANKING PAIR OF PILASTERS THAT TERMINATE WITH ICANTHUS-LEAF CAPITALS. **Right:** IN ADDITION TO FEATURING WOOD CARVED IN CLASSICAL MOTIFS, FIREPLACES OF THE EIGHTEENTH CENTURY WERE OFTEN PAINTED IN COLORS CHARACTERISTIC OF THE TIME: GREEN-GRAY, GRAY, GRAY-BLUE, AND BLUE.

Right: THE FRAGILE, GRACEFUL APPEAL OF THIS FIREPLACE'S APPLIQUÉD DESIGNS USING FRENCH PUTTY ARE AUGMENTED BY DECORATIVE INSETS OF BAS-RELIEF WEDGWOOD. **Below:** DRAWING ITS INSPIRATION FROM GREEK ARCHITECTURE, THE FEDERAL FIREPLACE WAS COMPARATIVELY SIMPLE, MAKING ITS DESIGN STATEMENT THROUGH EXCELLENT PROPORTIONS MORE THAN ELABORATE DECORATION.

Above: AMENABLE TO AN INTERIOR DESIGN THAT INCORPORATES ORNATE FURNISHINGS—INCLUDING SOME PERIOD FRENCH PIECES—THIS DELICATE FEDERAL PERIOD FIREPLACE, IN BASIC WHITE WITH CLASSICAL GREEK MOTIFS, SHOWS ENDURING VIABILITY AS AN IMPORTANT ARCHITECTURAL FEATURE.

Below: MORE FLAMBOYANT THAN THE EARLIER FEDERAL FIREPLACES, THOSE IN THE ROCOCO STYLE, WHEN MADE OF WOOD, FEATURED EXUBERANT CARVINGS THAT OFTEN TOOK FLORAL FORM AS GARLANDS AND BOUQUETS.

Above: THE CURVACEOUSNESS AND FREE FORM OF ITS CARVINGS AND APPLIQUED DESIGNS DISTINGUISH THE ROCOCO FIREPLACE FROM THE MORE GEOMETRIC, LINEAR NEOCLASSICAL DESIGNS.

Below: IN THE ROCOCO STYLE, MARBLE IS A FAVORITE MATERIAL FOR THE FIREPLACE FACING (THE OUTER MATERIAL DIRECTLY FACING THE FIREBOX, WHERE THE FIRE ACTUALLY BURNS) WITH AN ELABORATELY CARVED WOODEN MANTEL EXTENDING PAST IT AS A SOURCE OF DECORATION.

Above: THE FRENCH FIREPLACE DOESN'T HAVE TO BE OSTENTATIOUS IN TERMS OF DESIGN AND MATERIALS, BUT CAN TAKE MORE SUBTLE EXPRESSION AS EXEMPLIFIED BY THIS GENTLY CURVED, MODERATELY CARVED EXAMPLE.

Above left: ONE OF THE MOST ORNATE AND VISUALLY BUSY FORMS OF VICTORIAN ARCHITECTURE TAKES ITS CUES FROM GOTHIC DESIGN, FEATURING LATTICEWORK CARVINGS, TURNED PIECES, MULTIPLE EXTENSIONS, POINTED FINIALS, AND A COMBINATION OF MORE THAN ONE TYPE OF WOOD, AS SEEN ON THIS FIREPLACE.

Above right: DESPITE THE RELATIVELY SMALL SCALE OF MOST VICTORIAN ROOMS, VICTORIAN FIREPLACES WERE OFTEN DISPROPORTIONATELY LARGE, USING MASSIVE AMOUNTS OF HEAVILY CARVED OR PANELED WOOD.

Right: Hand-glazed (but unpatterned) tiles gained popularity as fireplace building materials during the Arts and Crafts Movement, which was a rebuttal, of sorts, to the machine-made products of the Industrial Revolution and the ornamental excesses of Victoriana. Arts and Crafts designers used traditional methods and materials to produce simple, clean designs.

Above: NATURAL MATERIALS SUCH AS FIELDSTONE, ESSENTIALLY UNPRETENTIOUS AND UNDECORATED, CHARACTERIZED SOME ARTS AND CRAFTS FIREPLACES, GIVING THEM A RUSTIC LOOK IN WHICH BEAUTY IS FOUND IN THE MATERIALS AND WORKMANSHIP, RATHER THAN IN ELABORATE ORNAMENTATION.

Left: WITH ITS SOLID PRESENCE AND PROPORTIONS AND STRAIGHTFORWARD DESIGN, THIS SUBSTANTIAL WOOD FIREPLACE WORKS WELL WITH THE MISSION FURNITURE AND CONTEMPORARY PIECES THAT GRACE THIS HOME. MISSION FURNITURE WAS THE AMERICAN EXPRESSION OF ARTS AND CRAFTS PRINCIPLES.

Right: IN ITS EXPLORATION OF NATURAL MATERIALS
AND CELEBRATION OF HANDCRAFTSMANSHIP, THE ARTS AND CRAFTS MOVEMENT
REVOLUTIONIZED DESIGN. IN THIS FIREPLACE, HAND-HAMMERED COPPER HAS
BEEN INCORPORATED INTO THE FIREPLACE DESIGN TO GREAT EFFECT, WITH AN
INSCRIPTION **(Above)** WORKED INTO THE COPPER. SUCH EXPRESSIONS OF THE
MOVEMENT'S CREDO WERE VERY POPULAR ELEMENTS OF FIREPLACES BUILT
DURING THE ARTS AND CRAFTS PERIOD.

Below: IN DRAMATIC CONTRAST TO THE STARK WHITE WALLS OF THIS CONTEMPORARY ROOM, THE DARK SLATE FIREPLACE SOARS IN A THREE-TIERED GEOMETRIC SCALE UP THE WALL, PAST CLERESTORY WINDOWS.

Above: STRIPPED OF CARVING AND ANY SUPERFLUOUS DECORATIVE DETAILING, FIREPLACES AFTER THE BAUHAUS STYLE OF MODERN ARCHITECTURE RELY ON MATERIALS AND FORM TO MAKE A DESIGN STATEMENT. THIS FIREPLACE IS PURE GEOMETRICS: OVERLAPPING VERTICAL AND HORIZONTAL RECTANGLES FLANKED BY STORAGE SPACE FOR A PERFECT COMBINATION OF PRACTICALITY AND GOOD LOOKS.

Above: Without a whit of decorative detailing, this fireplace reinterprets the traditional concept of a mantelpiece, jutting out from the wall in a sheer plane with rounded corners. The mantelshelf, thus, need not cantilever over the mantel but is simply the top of the mantelpiece itself.

Above: THIS CONTEMPORARY MARBLE FIREPLACE CONTRASTS WITH THE ENVELOPING WHITE OF THE WALLS TO BECOME AN IMPORTANT ARCHITECTURAL FEATURE OF THE ROOM. CUT IN TWO BAS-RELIEF GEOMETRIC FORMS ABOVE THE FIREBOX, WHERE A MANTELSHELF WOULD NORMALLY APPEAR, THE FIREPLACE ENCOURAGES THE VIEWER TO RETHINK OLDER ARCHITECTURAL CONCEPTS. **Right:** DEVOID ENTIRELY OF A MANTELPIECE, THIS FIREPLACE GAINS ITS STRIKING LOOKS WITH A GLOSSY MARBLE HEARTH CUT IN AN IRREGULAR SHAPE AND A COPPER HOOD THAT DESCENDS FROM THE CEILING, TERMINATING AT THE SPACE NORMALLY OCCUPIED BY A MANTELSHELF.

Above: ECHOING THE BUILDING MATERIALS OF THE HOME IT WARMS, THIS MODERN FIREPLACE REINVENTS THE NOTION OF SHEER GLASS WITH AN ALL-GLASS FIREBOX, TOPPED BY A STAIRSTEP RECTANGULAR TOWER LEADING TO THE HIGH CEILING AND THE CHIMNEY BEYOND. **Left:** IN A MASTERFUL STATEMENT OF MINIMALISM, THE CONTEMPORARY FIREPLACE SHOWN HERE IS A SIMPLE RECTANGLE CUT INTO THE WALL, WITH NO ADDITIONAL MATERIALS OR DECORATION GRACING IT AT ALL. THE IMPACT COMES FROM THE OFF-CENTER PLACEMENT OF THE FIREPLACE AT THE FAR CORNER OF THE WALL.

Regional Warmth

In addition to dating a home to a period or emulating a historic architectural style, the fireplace is often also an expression of regional design. As one of the home's major interior architectural features, the fireplace can set the whole mood or prevailing style of a room. Indeed, fireplaces can vary greatly from one part of the world to another when constructed with indigenous materials and designed according to a region's prevailing style.

There's no mistaking the Pueblo fireplace design of the American Southwest, with its unadorned white plaster or pale, earth-colored adobe that is so starkly simple, either linear or curved, that it's almost contemporary in appearance. Nor is there little doubt that the towering, sometimes walk-in, fieldstone fireplaces with rustic beams as mantelshelves point to the architecture of the Adirondacks Great Camps—a style repeated in mountainous rustic environments throughout the world. And, thanks to Frank Lloyd Wright's prairie style of architecture, even the American Midwest displays a regional style at the hearth, with fireplaces made from indigenous stones, carefully cut and finished into perfect rectangles.

When the goal is to build a home that reflects its site, the fireplace is an important communication tool. At the same time, the fireplace, as a regional indicator, can also be designed to bring a bit of another favorite region into the home, even when the home's actual location is somewhere else—thus, the fireplace of the popular American Southwestern style may show up as far away as Australia.

Above: SPANISH ARCHITECTURE HAS SPAWNED A FIREPLACE STYLE THAT IS TEXTURAL, CURVACEOUS, AND CLEAN. THIS FREESTANDING CUP-SHAPED EXAMPLE FEATURES A CLASSIC SPANISH (WITH MOORISH ORIGINS) ARCHED FIREBOX AND A HIGHLY TEXTURAL WHITEWASHED FINISH THAT GIVES THE FIREPLACE A STRIKING PRESENCE. Left: A TRANSITIONAL APPROACH THAT MERGES PUEBLO STYLE WITH TRADITIONAL FIREPLACE ARCHITECTURE CHARACTERIZES THIS FIREPLACE, SETTING THE THEME FOR THE ROOM'S DECOR OF BLENDED STYLES.

Right: MIMICKING PUEBLO ARCHITECTURE WITH ITS STRONG LINES AND UTTER SIMPLICITY, THIS FIREPLACE ANNOUNCES SOUTHWESTERN STYLE WITH CLEAR AUTHORITY. WITH THE MANTEL DIVIDED INTO TWO UNEQUAL LEDGES, ECHOING THE ARCHITECTURE OF THE ROOM, THE FIREPLACE HAS AN EXTRA EDGE OF EXCITEMENT.

Above: ALTHOUGH NO AUTHENTIC PUEBLO FIREPLACES TOOK THIS ARROW-TIP, CUTOUT FORM, THE ESSENCE OF THE ARCHITECTURAL STYLE IS CAPTURED IN THE FIREPLACE'S UNADORNED ADOBE-COLORED PLASTER, WHICH IS THEN CUT INTO GEOMETRIC RAYS REMINISCENT OF NATIVE AMERICAN DESIGN MOTIFS. **Right:** AS INTERESTING AS THE KIVA FIREPLACE IS IN ITS OWN RIGHT, ITS LOCATION SMACK IN THE MIDST OF KITCHEN COUNTERTOPS, SOARING THROUGH AND ABOVE THEM WITH STRIKING GRACE, UNDERSCORES ITS DRAMA.

Above: REINTERPRETED TODAY, THE FIELDSTONE FIREPLACE OF THE LODGE STYLE MAY BE SCALED DOWN AND MORE FINISHED SO THAT IT WORKS IN SMALLER CONTEMPORARY SPACES THAT NONETHELESS GAIN WARMTH WITH A SENSE OF RUGGEDNESS AND NATURAL GOOD LOOKS. **Left:** THE TURN-OF-THE-CENTURY LODGES BUILT AMID THE NATURAL BEAUTY OF AMERICA'S MOUNTAIN REGIONS, LIKE THIS ONE IN YELLOWSTONE NATIONAL PARK, PRODUCED A UNIQUE AND LASTING ARCHITECTURAL STYLE OF RUSTICITY AND EXPANSIVENESS, RELYING ON INDIGENOUS STONES, TWIGS, AND TIMBERS. FIREPLACES IN THESE LODGES WERE FIELDSTONE CONSTRUCTIONS THAT TOWERED ENORMOUSLY IN THE CENTRAL LODGE ROOM, IMPARTING ENVELOPING HEAT.

Above: CHARCOAL-COLORED STONE TOPPED WITH AN OLD BEAM AS MANTELSHELF CREATES AN APPROPRIATELY MASCULINE, NO-NONSENSE LOOK FOR THE INCREASINGLY POPULAR WESTERN OR COWBOY SCHOOL OF DESIGN.

Right: IN THIS RUSTIC CONTEMPORARY ARCHITECTURE, A COBBLESTONE FIREPLACE RECALLS THE ADIRONDACKS LODGE STYLE WITH ITS MASSIVE WIDTH AND HEIGHT.

Left: As an architect from the American Midwest, Frank Lloyd Wright brought a restraint and moderation characteristic of the region into his designs, as exemplified by this fireplace delineated by only a single brick's width—with the brick turned on end for a truncated look.

Above: In another example of Frank Lloyd Wright's breathtakingly creative approach to design, smooth-cut stones are given one-of-a-kind personality on this fireplace with a bas-relief carved abstract design that functions as modern art.

Below: SET ON END, THE FIREPLACE BRICKS SHOWN HERE CREATE A LINEAR PATTERN THAT COMPLEMENTS THE GEOMETRY EXPRESSED IN THE NATURAL WOOD OF THE HOME'S CRAFTSMAN ARCHITECTURAL STYLE.

Above: FARMHOUSES IN THE AMERICAN MIDWEST AT THE TURN OF THE CENTURY EXPRESSED A STRAIGHTFORWARD SENSIBILITY CARRIED THROUGH IN THEIR FIREPLACES, WHICH WERE OFTEN CLEAN WOOD AND GLAZED-TILE CONSTRUCTIONS INFLUENCED BY THE PRACTICAL AESTHETIC OF THE ARTS AND CRAFTS MOVEMENT.

Above: CONTEMPORARY AND TRADITIONAL ARCHITECTURAL STYLES MERGE IN THIS FIREPLACE DESIGN, WHICH FEATURES A SLEEK CONTEMPORARY FIREBOX TOPPED WITH A SHEER GLASS MANTELSHELF, FLANKED ON EITHER SIDE BY TRADITIONAL PILASTERS THAT FORM PART OF THE ROOM'S PANELING.

WHIMSY AND ART

Although our love of a fire may be both profound and serious, the fireplace itself can be pure fun. In the hands of creative homeowners, designers, architects, and artists, fireplaces can serve as the most exuberant style statements in the home. They can take flights of fancy with exotic faux finishes or bold color combinations and unique decorative paint treatments. Or they can feature unusual building materials such as shiny metal or mirror or even dyed stone. Even the very form of the fireplace—the basic rectangle—can be rethought in these innovative designs, becoming a triangle or perhaps a tiny circle much like the opening to a birdhouse. Practical matters such as a good draw aren't necessarily as important to these designs; rather, it's the artistry that counts. For the homeowners who enjoy them, these whimsical, dramatic, or otherwise innovative fireplaces are a telling sign of their own aesthetic sensibilities, as personal as a handprint.

Above: TEXTURE AND MATERIALS ARE THE KEY TO THIS CONTEMPORARY FIREPLACE, WHICH DRAWS ITS SINGULAR STYLING FROM EARTHY STONE JUXTAPOSED WITH A SLEEK, METALLIC CROWN.

Left: ZENLIKE IN ITS PARED-DOWN LINES AND RELIANCE ON POSITIVE AND NEGATIVE SPACE, THIS GRAY-TILED FIREPLACE STANDS IN A STATE OF GRACE AMID A ROOM FURNISHED IN EQUALLY SERENE, STILL BEAUTY.

Below: THE CLEAN, WHITE LINES OF CONTEMPORARY DESIGN THAT GIVE THIS FIREPLACE ITS DISTILLED QUALITY ARE ACCENTUATED BY A DARK-PAINTED MANTELSHELF ASYMMETRICALLY BRACKETED ON ONLY ONE SIDE.

Above: CONCEIVED IN TERMS OF THE ROOM'S OVERALL ARCHITECTURE AND DESIGN, THIS SPARE FIREPLACE GAINS WHIMSICAL CHARM WHEN TOPPED, UNEXPECTEDLY, WITH A MANTELSHELF BOASTING A FOLK-ART PIG ABOVE THE FIREBOX. THE FIREPLACE VIEW IS FRAMED LIKE ART BY THE DECORATIVE LINES OF THE WALLS, WHICH SERVE AS A WINDOW FROM THE ADJOINING SPACE INTO THE HEARTH. **Left:** THE HORIZONTAL PLANES THAT DEFINE THIS ROOM'S ARCHITECTURE AND FURNISHINGS ARE REPEATED IN ITS FIREPLACE—A SMALL, RECTANGULAR NICHE CARVED INTO THE FLOWING, HORIZONTAL WHITE OF THE WALL.

Right: WHEN CREATIVITY KNOWS NO BOUNDS, THE CONCEPT OF A FIREPLACE CAN TAKE ON A NEW DEFINITION. HERE, IT HAS KNOCKED DOWN WALLS, STANDING ON ITS OWN AS AN OPEN-FACED STOVE HIGHLIGHTED BY TWIN GEOMETRIC SHAPES IN THE CUT WALL BEHIND AND THE PLATFORM BELOW. **Below:** IN A CONTEMPORARY ROOM THAT'S A WORK OF ART, FURNISHED WITH ONLY THREE PIECES, EVERY ELEMENT MUST CARRY ITS WEIGHT AS A DESIGN STATEMENT. THIS ONE-OF-A-KIND FIREPLACE SUCCEEDS, WITH ITS SIMPLE, SQUARE FORM OUT-LINED BY CHARCOAL STROKES SUGGESTIVE OF MANTEL AND CHIMNEY.

Left: THE INTERNATIONAL STYLE, WITH ITS HARD GEOMETRIC EDGES AND ABSENCE OF DECORATIVE EMBELLISHMENT, PRODUCED A FIREPLACE THAT IS ESSENTIALLY LINEAR AND UNADORNED, WITH THE CRISP FORM OF THE FIREPLACE AND FLUSH PLANES OF THE RECTANGULAR FIREBOX SERVING AS AESTHETIC STATEMENTS IN THEIR OWN RIGHT. IN THIS SPARE LIVING ROOM WITH ITS BLOCKS OF STRONG COLOR, THE FIREPLACE MAKES A POWERFUL IMPRESSION.

Above: TAKING THE FORM OF A BUILDING FACADE, THIS VIBRANT RED FIREPLACE NODS TO MEXICAN AND MODERN INFLUENCES—THE RESULT IS SHEER FUN.

Above: EVEN THE MOST TRADITIONAL WOOD FIREPLACE MANTEL CAN GAIN UNEXPECTED VERVE

WHEN THE FIREPLACE FACING FEATURES A TOUCH OF PATTERN AND CONTRASTING COLOR.

Right: AN EXQUISITELY EXECUTED FAUX MARBLE FINISH, A CENTURIES-OLD DESIGN PLOY,

IMBUES THIS EIGHTEENTH-CENTURY-STYLE FIREPLACE WITH A DECORATIVE CHARACTER APPROPRIATE

FOR THE SPACE'S PERIOD FURNISHINGS.

Above: TAKING ITS INSPIRATION FROM AN AMISH QUILT, THIS FIREPLACE FEATURES A PATCHWORK OF RICHLY GLAZED, MULTIFARIOUS TILES CROWNED WITH A TRADITIONAL MANTEL.

Right: THE ERSTWHILE GRACE OF A VICTORIAN FIREPLACE WITH A MIRRORED MANTELPIECE EARNS A RIVETING RE-INSPECTION WITH A FIREPLACE FACING MADE OF BRIGHTLY COLORED CERAMIC SHARDS LAID IN A FREE-FORM MOSAIC. **Below:** RANDOMLY CUT BLACK–AND–WHITE TILE PROVIDES A FOCAL POINT FOR THIS FIREPLACE WHILE BLENDING HARMONIOUSLY WITH THE ROOM'S ABIDING UNDERSTATEMENT.

Above: WITH ITS RUSTIC PAINTED BRICK AND NO-NONSENSE WOODEN MANTELPIECE,

THIS HUMBLE FARMHOUSE STYLE FIREPLACE MAKES FOR AN INVITING HEARTH.

Left: A MELLOW, OLD WORLD AMBIANCE IS ACHIEVED WITH THIS FIREPLACE,

A SIMPLE ARCH PAINTED WEDGWOOD BLUE AND OUTLINED IN GOLD THAT IS INTEGRATED

INTO A WALL SPONGED WITH FADING TONES OF GOLD AND AMBER.

Above: WITH ITS CUSTOM TILEWORK EXTENDING TO THE HEARTH, THIS FIREPLACE COMPLETES THE VARIETY OF

PATTERNS IN THIS COZY FAMILY ROOM; ITS EARTHY TONES ENHANCE THE ROOM'S FEELINGS OF WARMTH AND VITALITY.

Right: DECORATIVE FURBELOWS AT THE FIREPLACE CAN TAKE ANY FORM, AS SHOWN BY THE FOUR FLORAL APPLIQUÉ

PANELS RISING ABOVE THIS HUMBLE BRICK FIREPLACE, GIVING IT A UNIQUE COTTAGE CHARM.

Above: A COUNTRY FRENCH FIREPLACE WITH A PICKLED FINISH GIVES A HOMEY, LIVED-IN LOOK OF YESTERYEAR

TO THIS ROOM WITHOUT BEING HEAVY-HANDED OR DETRACTING FROM THE LIGHT, COTTAGE FEELING.

Left: A MELANGE OF DECORATIVE TREATMENTS LENDS A WHIMSICAL AIR TO THIS FIREPLACE, FROM THE MUTED, SPONGED

WOOD WITH CLASSICAL DENTIL MOLDING TO THE PATTERNED, GLAZED TILES THAT COORDINATE WITH A COLLECTION

OF DELFTWARE. A *TROMPE L'OEIL* MURAL OF TREETOPS PAINTED ON THE UPPER WALL DIRECTLY ABOVE THE

MANTELPIECE COMPLETES THE ONE-OF-A-KIND VISION.

Above left: CONCEIVED AS A PIECE OF FOLK ART, THIS COUNTRY FIREPLACE FEATURES FAUX FINISHING TO RESEMBLE CARVED STONE. **Above right:** THE ECLECTIC ASSEMBLAGE OF FURNISHING STYLES IN THIS ROOM IS GROUNDED BY THE ARCHITECTURAL STATEMENT OF THE FIREPLACE, WHICH GIVES A CONTEMPORARY, GEOMETRIC TWIST TO A TRADITIONAL FORM USING UNLIKELY CEMENT BLOCKS. **Right:** FIRE TAKES ON SPECIAL EFFECTS WHEN THE TRADITIONAL APPROACH TO MANTEL AND CHIMNEY IS DISCARDED IN FAVOR OF A PLAIN CONCRETE FACING AND MANTELPIECE BISECTED WITH AN OPAQUE GLASS TOWER THAT FLICKERS AND GLOWS LIKE STAINED GLASS IN SUNLIGHT.

Left: BLUE AND WHITE CERAMIC TILES LAID ON THE DIAGONAL CREATE DYNAMIC RHYTHM

THROUGH PATTERN AND COLOR ON THIS FIREPLACE. **Above:** COLOR AND FORM,

A STRONG STATEMENT SPARINGLY ARTICULATED, MAKE THIS MORE THAN A FIREPLACE—IT IS

A WORK OF MODERN ART UPON THE CANVAS OF WHITE, CONTEMPORARY WALLS.

SOURCES

Designers

(pages 2; 37)
Michael Dale
Houston, TX
(713) 529-7102

(page 10)
Paula Viera, graphic
    designer
Newburyport, MA
(508) 462-9325

(page 15, bottom)
Stephen Huneck
Johnsbury, VT
(802) 748-5593

(page 17)
Clare Fraser Interior Design
New York, NY
(212) 737-3479

(page 19)
Elizabeth Speert Interiors
Watertown, MA
(617) 926-3725

(page 20, left)
Clara Hayes Barrett Interiors
Hingham, MA
(617) 749-5876

(page 23, right)
Annie Kelly
Los Angeles, CA
(213) 876-8030

(page 26)
David Livingston Interior
    Design
San Francisco, CA
(415) 392-2465

(pages 30, left; 52; 53)
Brian Murphy
Santa Monica, CA
(310) 459-0955

(page 30, right)
Rosenblum/Harb Architects
New York, NY
(212) 645-7474

(page 31)
Lori Erenberg
Pacific Palisades, CA
(310) 459-1515

(page 32)
Robert Wine
Birmingham, MI
(810) 642-2317

(page 34)
Koning/Eizenberg Architects
Los Angeles, CA
(310) 828-6131

(page 35)
Jack Brown
Bloomfield Hills, MI
(810) 646-8877

(page 36)
Roberto Redo
El Dorado Two Thousand
Mexico

(page 38, right)
George Padilla
Pasadena, CA
(213) 254-0636

(page 39)
Tom Callaway
Los Angeles, CA
(310) 828-1030

(page 41)
Schwartz/Silver Architects
Boston, MA
(617) 542-6650

(page 42)
Barbara Barry
Los Angeles, CA
(310) 276-9977

(page 48; front cover)
Barry Berkus
Santa Barbara, CA
(805) 963-8901

(pages 49; 67; 69)
Steven Ehrlich
Santa Monica, CA
(310) 828-6700

(page 50)
Goshow Associates
New York, NY
(212) 242-3735

(page 51, left)
Taft Architects
Houston, TX
(713) 522-2988

(page 51, right)
Sharon Campbell
San Anselmo, CA
(415) 453-2323

(page 54)
Frank Israel, architect
Los Angeles, CA
(310) 652-8087

(page 55)
Ace Architects
Oakland, CA
(510) 452-0775

(page 56)
Janet Johnson
Janet Allen Interiors
Plymouth, MA
(508) 746-1414

(page 58, right)
Larry Totah
Los Angeles, CA
(213) 467-2927

(page 59)
Louann Bauer
San Francisco, CA
(415) 621-7262

(pages 60; 64)
Charles Riley
New York, NY
(212) 206-8395

(page 62)
Richard Banks
San Francisco, CA
(415) 863-6162

(page 65)
Ellen O'Neill
New York, NY
(212) 318-7254

(page 66, right)
Mimi London
Los Angeles, CA
(310) 855-2567

(page 68)
Jarrett Hedborg
Los Angeles, CA
(310) 271-1437

Photography Credits

©Balthazar Korab: pp. 32, 35
©Mark Citret: p. 40
©Grey Crawford: pp. 25, 31, 38 top & bottom, 46 left, 49, 67, 69
©Derrick & Love: pp. 17, 50
©Feliciano: p. 57
©Michael Garland: pp. 48, 66 right
©Tria Giovan: pp. 20 right, 21, 60, 64
©Mick Hales: pp. 15 top, 22 right, 63
©David Henderson/Eric Roth Studios: p. 10
©Nancy Hill: p. 18 left
©Image/Dennis Krukowski: p. 36
©Jennifer Levy/Courtesy of Conde Nast Publications: p. 67
©David Livingston: pp. 26, 47, 51 right, 55, 59, 61, 62
©Randy O'Rourke: pp. 24 right, 58 left
©Peter Paige: pp. 2, 37

©David Phelps: pp. 28, 29
©Paul Rocheleau: pp. 13, 15, 16, 18 right, 22 left, 23 left
©Eric Roth: pp. 6, 9, 15 bottom, 19, 20 left, 56
©Richard Sexton: pp. 24 left, 43
©Tim Street-Porter: pp. 23 right, 30 left, 33, 34, 39, 42, 44, 45, 46 right, 52, 53, 54, 58 right, 66 left, 68
©Jessie Walker Associates: p. 27
©Paul Warchol: pp. 30 right, 41, 51 left

INDEX